new 100
Chat-Up Lines

IDEAS UNLIMITED (PUBLISHING)

Published by:
Ideas Unlimited (Publishing)
P.O. Box 125, Portsmouth
Hampshire PO1 4PP

ISBN: 1 871964 202

Limericks by Liz Garrad & Michael Walsh

Printed in UK

*Dedicated to all
the girls
I have known.*

INTRODUCTION

Have you ever clocked that perfect person across a crowded room, and just KNEW that you had to get to know her better. Picture the scene; your mouth goes dry, your knees start to shake, your hands begin to sweat, and your heart is beating so fast that you wonder if it's time to call the paramedics.

What is the cause of this strange phenomenon? It is certainly not something you have eaten or drunk, it is more likely that you are experiencing the magical emotion known to man since time began... LOVE,

So now what do you do? You have to talk to this person, but every line you ever knew has just popped out of your head. Relax – help is at hand. Just pop this little book into your back pocket, and success is guaranteed, well almost!!!

Throughout history men and women have gone to great lengths to make complete asses of themselves in order to meet. I guess with a book like this, things will now be somewhat different. Men and women can now look forward to making complete asses of themselves in style.

... And if this book helps to bring a smile to a few faces, or even succeeds to join two people together, then it hasn't been a complete waste of time.

ACKNOWLEDGEMENTS

I like to thank everyone who has helped to make this book possible. I am grateful to Liz garrad and Michael Walsh for their witty and clever limericks which as always are a pleasure to read.

Willy Sanker whose clever cartoons add spice to the subject of chatting up, and captures those moments we all know so well.

I like to thank the writers and poets, in particular those of the 16th and 17th century, whose work have inspired me, and some of which I have adapted to fit the realm of this book.

CONTENTS

CONTENTS

Go over to a blonde girl who has caught your eye and say;:

> *" They say blondes have the hottest kisses"*

Then show her the water pistol, or one of those small battery operated fans and say,

> *" But don't worry I come prepared."*

Go over to the angel you've just seen, and say;

"I must have died and gone to heaven, because I have never seen an Angel like you in here before."

Try this one for her sense of pity,

> *"I have to say I am sorry;*
> *And apologise to you;*
> *For being so darned ugly,*
> *That I never get to woo.*
>
> *A girl as sweet and pretty,*
> *As undoubtedly you are;*
> *If only I were handsome, Oh,*
> *Well then we might go far.*
>
> *But if we were together,*
> *So that people might relate;*
> *It would enhance your beauty,*
> *When compared with your new mate."*

Disco/Bar 4

Go over and say;

"Hi little miss dynamite, can I light your fuse?"

Party/Bar Etc. 5

Looking confident go over and say;

"God and fate are wondrous,
Their mysteries so unfold –
And that's why I approach you;
As fate and hope makes bold –

Yes, fate brought us together,
And it's easy to see why –
You are a little dolly bird,
And I'm a sexy guy."

If she looks as though she is trying to look intelligent, then
trick her into submission;

> *"Hi – I have been watching you*
> *I've done nothing else all night*
> *you're sexy and you're gorgeous*
> *I can tell you're really bright*
> *It's true – I'm very rarely wrong*
> *so something's puzzling me*
> *if you're really graced with perfect taste*
> *why aren't you dating me."*

This one is for the very brave.......Go over to her, give her
10p and say,

*"Here's 10p, call your mum and tell her you will
not be back till morning."*

If all else fails confuse them into surrender;

"Is it true that women always say the opposite of what they mean"

She'll reply: Yes/No

Then continue:

MMMM fascinating... Can I buy you a drink?

She'll reply: Yes/No

Then say;

"Good, what would you like."

> *"Perhaps if we could meet again,*
> *Perhaps – who knows, what might*
> *Be yours and mine, beyond the wine –*
> *Together in the night."*

If you see her everyday and have fallen for her, then tell her;

> *"We have travelled miles together*
> *I watch you every day*
> *and I'd really like to talk to you*
> *but don't know what to say*
> *if you've ever noticed me*
> *you haven't – there's no doubt*
> *but just in case you have well tell me –*
> *can I take you out?"*

Party/Night Club   **11**

Looking madly in love, go over and tell her,

"When I saw you my heart stood still, mind you the rest of me started to tremble, and kick up quite a fuss. So much so that I am now in agony. So how about you helping me ease the pain."

Train/Public Transport

This one is for those who have broken up but wish to go back together,

> *"I scanned your picture, dreaming,*
> *Till each dear line and hue*
> *Was imaged, to my seeming,*
> *As if it lived anew.*
>
> *Your lips began to borrow*
> *their former wondrous smile;*
> *Your fair eyes, faint with sorrow,*
> *Grew sparkling as estwhile.*
>
> *Such tears as often ran not*
> *Ran then, my love, for thee;*
> *And O, believe I cannot*
> *That thou art lost to me."*

Adapted from a poem by Rudyard Kipling

Party 13

Go up to the girl and whilst pulling out a tube of super glue out of your pocket, say,

"If you think that men and women should form a lasting bond, then come and stick with me kid."

Night Club 14

Go over looking her straight in the eyes, and say;

"Please don't do that"

To which she will probably reply;

"What?"

Then continue by saying;

"Raise your eyelids like that, its as if you are taking off all you clothes. Those eyes were not meant to be seen like that. So either stop it or I'll report you for indecent exposure."

Pub/Party 15

If you are with your friends and see a girl you'd like to meet, then this might be appropriate,

> *"I love you more than I can say,*
> *I love you now – forever;*
> *I love you more than anything –*
> *My football, mates – whatever!"*

Disco/Night Club 16

This one is for that not so pretty girl

"You know someone once said that a man who won't lie to a woman has very little consideration for her feelings. So can I buy you a drink gorgeous?"

Pub/Party

Go over to her looking amazed and say,

"Forgive me for intruding like this, but I had to come over and congratulate you."

To which she will reply; "WHAT FOR?"

continue by saying,

"That is some reputation you have built for yourself around here. They say that you are one of those intelligent girls who doesn't fall for any old cheap chat up line, and that you are very choosy about the kind of guy you talk to. You are just the kind of girl I have been looking for to help me with my research for a new book entitled,

"THE UNATTAINABLE ROSE... A DYING BREED

"Can we discuss the royalties over a drink."

Party/Bar 18

Go over to the girl you like to meet, and stay quiet. Then a few minutes later tell her,

"True friendship comes when silence between two people is comfortable… I am fairly comfy, how about you?"

Proposal of Marriage 19

If she looks like the settling down type, then this could win her heart;

"Agile and slender – and pretty,
My heart has been won by your style,
If you find me handsome and daring,
Perhaps we shall walk down the aisle."

Night Club/Beach   20

Go over to a girl who looks half naked and say,

"That's a lovely dress you are almost wearing... I must tell You I am not against half naked girls... at least not as often as I'd like to be... Well?"

Night Club/Party   21

Looking very scared of a rejection, go over and recite;

"Am I making a mistake
I don't know what to say
'cause every time I look at you
you smile and look away
you must know that I like you
look – I'm shaking what a state!!
so put me out of misery agree to have a date."

If she is the really pretty type who also knows it, then try this;

> *"I fell in love with you but then,*
> *That's no surprise to you;*
> *Perhaps you'd like to be my date –*
> *And stay forever true."*

Discotheque/Party 23

Go over to her and say;

"Its good to find an intelligent looking girl around here. You know I too keep my brain in good shape... its my second favourite organ. Do you want to know about my favourite organ... you should... you are holding it, its my heart."

Go over to the girl with a rose in hand, stand in front of her and start talking to the rose saying,

"Now that is what a beautiful English rose should look like... Now go closer and learn."

Then give the girl the rose and say,

"This is my pet rose, would you take her and give her a few pointers on how to be truly beautiful... Meanwhile I'll get you a drink for your trouble... What will you have?"

Looking fairly official, go over to the girl dancing around her handbag, and say;

"Please pretend you know me. My name is John, I am one of the bouncers here. Apparently there is a guy wondering around eyeing girl's handbags, and we think it was him who ran off with one last week. Since you are one of the easy preys, dancing around your handbag, I have to stay close ready to catch him in action. We mustn't make it look suspicious, so do you mind if I buy you a drink…"

Go over and ask for help;

"...would you help me with my training?... I want to become a sex maniac... but keep failing the practical."

If the timing is not right, pass on this message to her;

> *"Fate has just decided*
> *that you should be with me*
> *it's powerful don't fight it*
> *because it is meant to be*
> *when you're not so busy*
> *then please feel free to call*
> *I've included my phone number*
> *why not give me a call"*

Name ....

Tel ....

Send her this note, and wait for the nod;

Here's the CV of a fool in love

Name ....

Age ....

Very Good looking
Rich, Tall, & Cute
Great sense of humour
Bubbly personality
Very sensitive
Cries watching Bambi
Extremely Generous
Highly intelligent
Always sincere even
when he doesn't mean it.

Can I come over for an interview?

Send her this note and wait for the nod;

*"Do you want to see the face
that goes with this body?"*

"Then just hold this card up and I'll be right over."

If you feel confident, then try this;

"I am drawn to you because of your sad beauty which has pierced my heart. And I feel very guilty that unless I intervene, then fickle fate will condemn you to a lifetime of drudgery and unhappiness as a mere play thing of someone less high minded than I, and altogether inferior to me in every aspect.
My act of charity is to offer myself and thus cheat fate whilst at the same time gain for myself the love and loyalty of a beautiful – and happier woman… What do you think?"

Here's one for the very brave...

"that's a nice blouse... I bet it would look even nicer hanging over the end of my bed."

Short but to the point;

> *"I'd like your hand upon my arm,*
> *Your ring upon my finger,*
> *I'd like your dress upon the floor –*
> *If you would like to linger."*

Write this on a serviette and pass it over to her;

*"You have captured my heart with your beauty
My future has just been unfurled;
With you I am ready for romance,
I'm ready to take on the world.*

*I dream of long walks in the meadows,
With you, only you by my side;
A partner for life's rich adventure,
Your heart linked with mine as our guide.*

*So smile if you share my opinion,
And smile once this cute card is read –
If you would wake up in the morning,
With your dress at the foot of my bed."*

Night Club/Party

Go over to the pretty girl and say;

*"I am very sexy, rich and extremely handsome....
and what's your excuse for being so irresistible?"*

Party/Night Club

Make sure she is a blonde with blue eyes;

> *"Your eyes are blue your hair is golden,*
> *Your skin is alabaster;*
> *If you refuse and I should lose,*
> *My life will spell disaster."*

Give her this note, if you can't talk to her there,

> *"I look out at the Stars each night*
> *I suffer – I'm in pain*
> *my heart it skips a beat each time*
> *I ever hear your name*
> *I need to get to know you*
> *though you're in each of my dreams*
> *but life ain't fair you don't know*
> *I love you – so it seems*
> *So take this card away with you*
> *I ask of you – that's all*
> *and if you'd like to talk to me*
> *then please give me a call."*

Name ....

Tel ....

For this one you need the help of an ugly guy. So find one, give him a fiva and ask him to go over to the girl you like to meet and start chatting her up.

Then a minute or two later go over and tap the guy on the shoulder and say,

"Can't you see the lady is not interested, so just go away."

Then get him to look at you as if he knew your reputation as a tough guy and say,

"Oh it's you..., I am sorry I didn't know she was with you.

Then as he walks away, look at her and say,

"Sometimes I am embarrassed to be a guy... Can I buy you a drink as an apology for idiots like that?"

Party/Night Club 38

Find a sporty girl to try this one on;

"Do you fancy coming up to my place for a spot of indoor sports?"

Party/Night-club 39

If all you care about is to just kiss her, then this little poem may give a hint.

"Give me a kiss and to that kiss a score
Then to that twenty add a hundred more
A thousand to that hundred, so kiss on
To make that thousand up a million
Treble that million and when that is done
Lets kiss afresh as when we first begun."

Beach/Park

She is the hottest thing on the beach, so go over and offer to cool her down.

"I realise that there is nothing more annoying when you are trying to have a lie in the sun when a complete idiot comes over and starts talking to you... But I thought I come over anyway, in case you liked complete idiots, specially those bearing gifts."

Then hand over the ice cream, and try to impress her before she is finished.

Why not get her to lie back and think of England...

"I represented England in the Sexual Olympics last year, Would you help me with my training for the next Olympics?"

This is for the most gullible looking girl you find;

"Hi I am doing some market research for a razor company.... Can you spare a few moments to help me?

All you have to do is to kiss me and tell me how smooth I am."

Trick her into your arms;

> *"Tell me is it really true*
> *Or is it just a rumour*
> *That girls who look as good as you*
> *Have got no sense of humour*
> *You can't have too much trouble*
> *When it comes to guys and scoring*
> *But if you won't come out with me*
> *Then I was right – You're boring."*

Here's one In case you get bored at the laundrette

"Listen I've got loads of cheek
but sadly not much dosh
and looking at the load you've got
you don't have much to wash
I've got some bits and pieces here
that I need to get clean
so why don't you and me
just share the cost of a machine
don't worry there is no danger
they'll get along just fine
and it's nice to think your underwear
is getting close to mine."

Laundrette

If he has been watching you, but hasn't built up the
courage, then help him out;

> *"Aright Pal come on now*
> *Please give me a break*
> *Despite you bought that tie to wear*
> *Today quite by mistake*
> *I have seen you watching me*
> *on and off all night*
> *Unless you are cross eyed that is*
> *You've been doing it all night*
> *I'm sad because it's time to go*
> *And we both have missed our chance*
> *so before the evening's over*
> *be brave and come and dance."*

Street 46

Use her love of cars to your advantage;

"I am like an antique car... I am unique, stylish and always get there very s l o w l y ... Do you want a little test drive?"

Restaurant/Bar 47

Go over to the girl sitting alone, and say;

"Excuse me are you waiting For someone?"

To which she will probably say

"YES"

Then continue by saying,

"Good, So am I... Can I buy you a drink while we wait for our friends to arrive.

Swimming Pool/Beach

If your prey is older than you, then this line may be appropriate, but before saying the last line, make sure you duck.

"You look stunning… You still have the body of a twenty year old, but I think you should give it back, you're getting it all wrinkled."

Party/Club

Go over to her looking as if you know her and say,

"Sorry to have been staring at you. I was wondering. Do you know

..(insert your name here)."

She will think carefully and finally say that she doesn't, at which point you can say,

"Would you like to."

Here's a request for a future date;

> *"You have left me speechless*
> *I don't know what to say*
> *I'm terrified that you might leave*
> *I can't stand that – no way*
> *You don't know my number*
> *And you don't know my name*
> *And if you go away my life*
> *Will never be the same*
> *So here it is please call me*
> *I'm shaking I can't wait*
> *To share a perfect evening*
> *With my perfect date."*

"O my love's like a red, red rose
That's newly sprung in June:
O my love's like the melody
That's sweetly played in tune.

As fair art thou, my bonnie lass,
So deep in love am I:
And I will love thee still, my dear,
Till a' the seas gang dry:

Till a' the seas gang dry, my dear,
And the rocks melt with the sun;
I will love thee still, my dear,
While the sands o' life shall run.

And fare thee weel, my only love!
And fare thee weel awhile;
And I will come again my love,
though' it were ten thousand mile."

R. Burns

Girls love to feel special

> *"Your eyes absorb my heart,*
> *And your heart enslaves my soul,*
> *To bend my knee to you and give,*
> *Is now my only goal."*

If she is looking bored in a laundrette, then amuse her;

> *"Stand there looking puzzled*
> *with the powder in your hand*
> *saying there are just some things*
> *a man can't understand*
> *I put my undies in the wash*
> *the same way as you do*
> *but somehow everything goes wrong*
> *and the whole lot turns out blue*
> *could you help me out this time*
> *as a favour do you think*
> *and while our stuff is drying*
> *we could go and have a drink."*

Take Away/Restaurant 54

Just hope she is on the menu;

"Hello little miss scrumptious... Are you for take away or to have here?"

Party/Bar 55

If you don't want to look silly after a rejection, then try this;

Boy: *Only fools, absolute morons and idiots would respond by saying no to this question – Can I buy you a drink?*

Girl: NO

Boy: *Only fools, absolute morons and idiots would respond by saying no to this question: Will you go out with me?*

Girl: NO

Boy: *I gave you two chances and you still gave yourself away.*

Then walk away and watch her follow you.

If the timing is not right, arrange to meet her later;

> *"I'm giving you this card*
> *and that is all I'll do tonight*
> *I don't know if you'll call me*
> *if you like me, you just might*
> *and if you don't well babe that's life*
> *I won't shed any tears*
> *but you should know*
> *that you're the best*
> *I've seen in here for years"*

Name ....

Tel ....

Only the brave guys should try this, Go over to her and ask:

"Tell me do you sleep on your front?"

She will probably say, "No"

Continue by saying,

"Do you mind if I do?"

Try this on the romantic looking girl,

> *"You are a lady sweet and kind*
> *was never face so pleased my mind*
> *I did but see you passing by*
> *and yet I love you till I die*
> *Give us a smile before we part*
> *and I'll keep it forever in my heart."*

Go over and talk as if you know what you are talking about;

"They say that a good sex life is essential if you want to keep young trim fit and healthy... now say "HI" to your new exercise machine."

"Excuse me, I couldn't help notice,
Your figure is perfect, divine;
You have a rare beauty,
You are a sweet cutie,
I wish, oh, I wish you were mine."

Gym/Keep Fit Classes

If she looks like the domesticated type, then try this;

> *"Excuse me can you help me*
> *I hope that you can too*
> *my Mum's coming to supper*
> *and I don't know what to do*
> *you seem to know the things to buy*
> *you know just where to look*
> *I'd bet my life that you are*
> *just a million dollar cook*
> *can you tell me what to serve*
> *so that mother will not moan*
> *about how I cannot feed myself*
> *and beg me to come home.*
> *You look just like the sort of girl*
> *who'll know just what to do*
> *and if you teach me properly*
> *next time I'll cook for you."*

Party/Club 62

If you have a slight belly, now is your chance to use it to your advantage. Go over looking sad and say;

"You know I used to have a fantastic physique until my stomach decided to go on a career of it own, now one look at you and my heart wants to leave home... can I talk to you about it over a drink?"

Park/Street 63

Give her a big beautiful bunch of flowers, and say

"Hold these close, cause I think beautiful things should always stick together."

"Could I hang around and watch you both in envy?"

You need to do a little bit of acting for this. Go over and say;

"They say the best way to bring someone out of a hypnotic trance is to kiss him on the cheek. I bet you have the kind of smile which would hypnotise any man on earth however strong willed he may be."

Then once she smiles… Pretend you are being hypnotised, and whilst say the following try to stay still;

"No please don't smile don't do d d d "

Appear hypnotised, stay still and wail for that kiss.

Party/Night Club 65

"At least have the decency to give me a ransom note."

to which she will probably reply: "What?"

continue by saying;

"You kidnapped my heart, and I am here to collect the ransom note. I will follow your instructions to the letter, whatever they may be."

Just hope that her instructions doesn't include you getting lost.

"If you and I were left, my love
If you and I were left
Would we start mankind, my love
Start the world afresh

If you and I were lost in space
If you and I were lost
Would we start talking some place
Start the world afresh

If you and I were left my love
my love what would we do?
I know, Lets just pretend, my love
And start the world afresh."

"Wow I must be dreaming
– oh pinch me I won't care
You looked like Pamela Anderson
when I was over there
but now I've got much closer
–I don't know what to think
'cause you're much better looking –
oh and would you like a drink"

She knows she looks nothing like Pamela, but if she thinks
that you do, then you are in luck."

This is for the girl who looks like a pet lover,

> *"I have a little dog at home,*
> *He's fun (a ball of fur);*
> *He hates it when I leave him,*
> *And it breaks my heart I swear,*
> *To leave him on his own at night,*
> *He thinks that I don't care.*
> *I know he'd love to meet you,*
> *He's so cute, his name is spot,*
> *He'd love to have you as a friend,*
> *Perhaps – No better not;*
> *I think you'll fall in love with him,*
> *You'll like him quite a lot."*

If you feel confident, then try this;

"I am very sexy, rich and extremely handsome....and what's your excuse for being so irresistible?"

If you have watched her say no to a few guys, here's your chance to try to be different;

"I am sorry for intruding, but this doesn't happen to me often... to see another MENSA member in a place like this. I noticed you brushing off the rift raf, waiting for an intelligent conversation and a tantalising company.... So I thought I come over for the rescue, what will you have to drink."

If you don't want to approach him in front of your friends, then lay the seeds for later;

> *"You really are my ideal man*
> *Your looks just leave me weak*
> *But we're packed in here like cattle*
> *everyone is cheek to cheek*
> *so later when it's quieter*
> *and the others have gone home*
> *Perhaps you'll have a drink with me*
> *and we can be alone"*

Party 72

Go over and push your luck with this one;

"Do you know what the best lovers have for breakfast????"

"Well this morning I had eggs, toast, orange juice…"

Go over and say;

"Do you want to talk about it?"

To which she will reply;

"About what?"

Then say;

"Why are you fighting it?"

"Fighting what?"

Then say;

"Why are you questioning it?"

She will reply;

"Questioning what?"

Then tell her;

"My pathetic attempt at meeting the girl of my dreams...

My name is ....What is yours?"

Chat Up Card 74

If you are not sure whether she is going to say yes or know; find out the easy way; give her a call card;

> *"Here's my card to show you I care*
> *I hope that you won't lose it*
> *my name and number's on there too*
> *so don't be shy – just use it."*

Bar/Night Club 75

Send her this note;

"Hello! I hope you don't mind me sending you this card. I am painfully conscious of the fact that I might be making a fool of myself. You see, all of my friends laugh at me and tell me that I am always doing or saying the wrong things. But I can't see how I can say anything wrong in one short paragraph. So how would like to come and sit on my knee and we will chat about the first thing that pops up?"

"Get your coat... you've pulled"

If you think she might reject you, then try this one;

> *"Sweet Heart I have had a sign*
> *a message from above*
> *it told me to come here tonight*
> *'cause I would find true love*
> *but I have searched this place for hours*
> *fruitlessly I fear*
> *so if you see my perfect woman*
> *can you tell her that I'm here."*

Party/ Bar 78

Go over to her looking kind of pitiful, and say

"Since you have taken my heart to play with, the rest of me wants to know if we can come and watch."

Park/Street 79

Take your dog and go over to the girl you like to meet and say:

"They say that a bore is a person who deprives you of your solitude without providing you with company... That's why I have brought my dog to keep you company, while I bore you by telling you what I wouldn't give for the chance to take you out."

Place of Work/College

If you want more that just a friendship with that special someone, the tell her;

> *"Every week I see you*
> *We get along it's true*
> *And I would really like to see*
> *More and more of you*
> *We share a sense of humour*
> *We get along just fine*
> *So why don't you come around sometime*
> *And share a glass of wine*
> *Everytime we say good-bye*
> *It's true I really miss you*
> *And what I really like to do*
> *Is finally just to kiss you"*

Are you feeling lucky, the try this;

> *"Hello babe don't fight it*
> *you know you want to kiss me*
> *the minute that I walk away*
> *I promise you you'll miss me"*

But don't be surprised if she replies by saying;

> *"You don't half love yourself*
> *and I feel I have to say*
> *if the last man left on earth were you*
> *I'd have no choice – I'd be gay."*

Supermarket

Hang around the freezer section of the supermarket. As soon as you see the person you would like to meet, go over to her and say,

"You know it's dangerous for you to be in this section, You are so hot you could melt all the food around here."

Night Club/Disco

If you have a beer gut, go over to her, and say;
(but be prepared for a clip round the ear).

"What do you get if you press a slim belly against a big fat belly?"

"I don't know either... Lets find out."

This is for those who want to appeal to her intellectual vanity,

> *"Heh, Heh, my little bright one;*
> *I see you have a brain,*
> *Discernment, academia,*
> *With culture so arcane.*
>
> *And so for you, my dearie,*
> *And so for you my sweet;*
> *Let's visit my apartment,*
> *For I have a little treat.*
>
> *I need your learned opinion,*
> *On my Rembrant, Monet too,*
> *My Degas and my Turner,*
> *Perhaps you'd like to view.*
>
> *I value your perception,*
> *Appreciate you're smart,*
> *Let's go upstairs and hear your views,*
> *On classic works of art."*

Party/Bar

She might think you are weird, but hey…

> *"I'm from planet Zob*
> *I arrived on earth today*
> *I'm working out your culture*
> *and I'm getting on OK.*
> *I've studied your intelligence*
> *And the speed of your reflexes*
> *But what you need to help me with*
> *Is the difference with the sexes!!"*

Night Club/Disco

If you see a girl sitting at the bar, go over and say,

"Why did the guy cross the dance floor?
Because he fell in love with girl at the bar."

Beg her for help with this one;

> *"I wish I was a prince again –*
> *Far better than a frog;*
> *Perhaps you'd like to wed a prince –*
> *Go on, let's have a snug."*

Go over to the girl you would like to meet and say,

"Are you one of those superficial girls who ignores a guy's sensuality, personality and good character, and judges him by how he looks?"

To which she will probably reply, "YES"

Then continue...

"Good...What do you think...?"

Go over looking very impressed and say,

"They say that the difference between beauty and charm is that a beautiful woman is one who I notice, and a charming woman is one who notices me... So I have come over to see if you are charming as well beautiful... Well?'

Go over and say,

"I bet you are one of those liberated women who thinks that men are like nappies...must be changed regularly, easily disposable and always full of shit. Well anyway my name is Pampy, can I buy you a drink?"

Try this one on the shy looking girl sitting on her own.

> *"Hey hello – don't hide your face*
> *it's really such a pity*
> *that you won't even look at me*
> *'cause your face is really pretty*
> *can we talk or take a walk*
> *do I have a chance*
> *well will you just hold on to me*
> *while we have a dance."*

Night Club/Bar 92

Girls always like to get top marks;

*"They say sex appeal is 50% what you've got and
50% what people think you've got... So how would
you like to bribe me for a full 100%?"*

Street/Shop 93

Looking really happy, go over and say,

*"You know what you've done don't you? You've
gone and challenged a myth. Legend has it that if
you're lucky at gambling then you will be unlucky
in love... but... well, I won the lottery last week,
and never dreamed that I could get lucky twice;
but now I have found you and have fallen madly
in love with you."*

Just stick around long enough for you to grow on her before
you confess it was only a tenner.

Go and invite her to a dinner party;

> *"Darling can you help me*
> *you look like you are kind*
> *I've really got a problem*
> *can you help me – would you mind*
> *I've got a dinner party*
> *it's tonight at eight you see*
> *and the only guy who hasn't got*
> *a partner well that's me*
> *so could you come along with me*
> *pretend to be my girl*
> *go on say you will – oh at least give it a whirl*
> *live dangerously for once –*
> *oh babe please give me a chance*
> *let's be friends and by tomorrow friendship might*
> *become romance.*

If you want to get you own back, this is for you;

> *"I've been watching you all evening*
> *I've tried to catch your eye*
> *but you won't come and dance with me*
> *and you won't tell me why*
> *you keep on giggling with your friend*
> *I thought that you had class*
> *so if you fancy kissing me*
> *well go on – here's my ass."*

Disco/Night Club

Go over to the guy who looks in pain, and cheer him up;

> *"Ooh you don't look very well*
> *your lips are awfully blue*
> *are you hurting badly*
> *tell me dear what did you do?*
> *is it a football injury*
> *or were you running on a track*
> *were you training in the gym*
> *and have you hurt your back*
> *oh you were in a night club then*
> *were you dancing – did you slip*
> *oh you were in the gents*
> *and you got WHAT caught in your zip."*

Go over and rely on her sense of pity;

"They say all you need to successfully chat up a beautiful girl is to be pitiful and confident... Well I am a pretty sad case, so just don't shatter my confidence, and we'll see if the saying is true."

Night Club/Bar   98

> *"I've been hit by cupids arrow*
> *And you are the one I see*
> *Tell me you've been hit by it too,*
> *And I am the one you see."*

Over the mountains
And over the waves,
Under the fountains
And under the graves;
under floods that are deepest,
Which Neptune obey;
Over rocks that are steepest
Love will find out the way.

You may esteem him
A child for his might,
Or you may deem him,
A coward from his flight;
But if she whom love doth honour
Be concealed from the day,
Set a thousand guards upon her
Love will find out the way.

Some think to lose him
By having him confined;
And some to suppose him,
Poor thing, to be blind;
But if ne're so close you wall him
Do the best that you may,
Blind love, if so you call him,
Will find out his way.

You may train the eagle
To stoop to your fist;
Or you may inveigle
The phoenix of the east;
The lioness, you may move her
To give over her prey;
But you'll never stop a lover:
He will find out his way.

Anon

Hold this book up to reveal the cover. Then while turning the pages as if you were looking for an appropriate line to use, say;

"No... I can't find one worthy of your beauty and charm, can I buy you a drink anyway?"

Telephone Numbers

Name ....

Telephone Number ....

Marks out of Ten ....

Name ....

Telephone Number ....

Marks out of Ten ....

Name ....

Telephone Number ....

Marks out of Ten ....

Telephone Numbers

Name ....

Telephone Number ....

Marks out of Ten ....

Name ....

Telephone Number ....

Marks out of Ten ....

Name ....

Telephone Number ....

Marks out of Ten ....

Telephone Numbers

Name ....

Telephone Number ....

Marks out of Ten ....

Name ....

Telephone Number ....

Marks out of Ten ....

Name ....

Telephone Number ....

Marks out of Ten ....

OTHER TITLES FROM IDEAS UNLIMITED (PUBLISHING)

copies "100 CHAT UP LINES" ....£ 1.99

copies "IDIOTS HANDBOOK OF LOVE & SEX"..........£ 1.99

copies "10 GOLDEN RULES OF CHATTING UP" ....£ 1.99

copies "SIZE ISN'T EVERYTHING"............................£ 1.99

copies "THE 9 SECOND SEX MACHINE" ....£ 1.99

copies "HOW TO WIN THE NATIONAL LOTTERY" ......£ 1.99

copies "NOT WON THE LOTTERY YET THEN?" ....£ 1.99

copies "SEX QUESTIONS & ANSWERS" ....£ 1.99

copies "HAVE YOU SEEN THE NOTICE BOARD?" ....£ 3.99

copies "SEEN THE NEW NOTICE BOARD?" ....£ 3.99

copies "SPORT FOR THE ELDERLY" ....£ 2.50

copies "BEGINNERS GUIDE TO KISSING"..................£ 2.50

copies "TIPS FOR A SUCCESSFUL MARRIAGE"..........£ 2.50

copies "THE JOY OF FATHERHOOD" ....£ 2.50

copies "OFFICE HANKY PANKY" ....£ 2.50

copies "BODY LANGUAGE SEX SIGNALS"..................£ 2.50

copies "WELL HUNG" ....£ 2.99

copies "OF COURSE I LOVE YOU" ....£ 1.99

copies "100 NEW CHAT UP LINES" £1.99

copies "THE BEST OF CHAT UP LINES" (key ring)......£2.99

copies "CHAT UP CARDS" (key ring) £2.99

copies "LOVE & PASSION FOR ELDERLY"..................£2.50

I have enclosed a cheque/postal order for £..........................
made payable to IDEAS UNLIMITED (PUBLISHING)

Name ....

Address ....

....

....

....

County ....Post Code...............................

Fill in the coupon above and send it with your payment to:

IDEAS UNLIMITED (PUBLISHING)
PO BOX 125, PORTSMOUTH, HAMPSHIRE, PO1 4PP

Postage FREE within the UK.

If you wish your purchase to be sent directly to someone
else(e.g.; Birthday, Christmas, Wedding, Valentines Gift),
simply fill in their name and address in the coupon above,
and enclose your cheque/postal order with your personal
message or card, if desired. We will be pleased to send your
gift directly to your chosen recipient.

OTHER TITLES FROM IDEAS UNLIMITED (PUBLISHING)

copies "100 CHAT UP LINES" ....£ 1.99

copies "IDIOTS HANDBOOK OF LOVE & SEX" ....£ 1.99

copies "10 GOLDEN RULES OF CHATTING UP" ....£ 1.99

copies "SIZE ISN'T EVERYTHING" ....£ 1.99

copies "THE 9 SECOND SEX MACHINE" ....£ 1.99

copies "HOW TO WIN THE NATIONAL LOTTERY" ....£ 1.99

copies "NOT WON THE LOTTERY YET THEN?" ....£ 1.99

copies "SEX QUESTIONS & ANSWERS" ....£ 1.99

copies "HAVE YOU SEEN THE NOTICE BOARD?" ....£ 3.99

copies "SEEN THE NEW NOTICE BOARD?" ....£ 3.99

copies "SPORT FOR THE ELDERLY" ....£ 2.50

copies "BEGINNERS GUIDE TO KISSING" ....£ 2.50

copies "TIPS FOR A SUCCESSFUL MARRIAGE" ....£ 2.50

copies "THE JOY OF FATHERHOOD" ....£ 2.50

copies "OFFICE HANKY PANKY" ....£ 2.50

copies "BODY LANGUAGE SEX SIGNALS" ....£ 2.50

copies "WELL HUNG" ....£ 2.99

copies "OF COURSE I LOVE YOU" ....£ 1.99

copies "100 NEW CHAT UP LINES" £1.99

copies "THE BEST OF CHAT UP LINES" (key ring)......£2.99

copies "CHAT UP CARDS" (key ring) £2.99

copies "LOVE & PASSION FOR ELDERLY" £2.50

I have enclosed a cheque/postal order for £............................
made payable to IDEAS UNLIMITED (PUBLISHING)

Name ....

Address ....

....

....

....

County ....Post Code...............................

Fill in the coupon above and send it with your payment to:

IDEAS UNLIMITED (PUBLISHING)
PO BOX 125, PORTSMOUTH, HAMPSHIRE, PO1 4PP

Postage FREE within the UK.

If you wish your purchase to be sent directly to someone
else(e.g.; Birthday, Christmas, Wedding, Valentines Gift),
simply fill in their name and address in the coupon above,
and enclose your cheque/postal order with your personal
message or card, if desired. We will be pleased to send your
gift directly to your chosen recipient.